New Songs of Innocence

More Praise for *New Songs of Innocence*

In *New Songs of Innocence*, S. J. Hodson's nuanced observations of nature yield a glimpse into the lives of trees, birds, squirrels, deer and cougars. Similarly, his poems record moments from his own life, in the kitchen, at war, and in love, providing a profound glimpse into the human condition.

Ené Lewis – a working artist since 1961.

=/=/=

Almost every morning for the past five years I have been waking to a new poem from Stan Hodson in my email inbox. Those poems — some of them collected here in *New Songs of Innocence* — set the tone for my day. Stan sees the world and everything in it with the eyes of a young child and a wise old man. His deep knowledge of physics and biology commingles with an understanding of human nature and an unusual personal history to create poems that startle, occasionally make me laugh out loud, and always make me think. Stan Hodson is one of our era's best poets.

Susan Bennerstrom – painter and celebrant of light,
www.susanbennerstrom.com

New Songs of Innocence

S. J. Hodson

St. Augustine's Press
South Bend, Indiana

Manufactured in the United States of America.

1 2 3 4 5 6 30 29 28 27 26 25

Library of Congress Control Number: 2025932156

Paperback ISBN: 978-1-58731-554-1
Ebook ISBN: 978-1-58731-555-8

∞ The paper used in this publication meets the minimum requirements of the American National Standard for Information Sciences – Permanence of Paper for Printed Materials, ANSI Z39.48-1984.

St. Augustine's Press
www.staugustine.net

This book is dedicated to Annie Dillard and to Tony Connor — keen writing coaches, and inspiring stewards of Literature.

Contents

Mineral

Vegetal

Personal

= / = / =

Acknowledgments

Movement in a Solid

was selected by poet Richard Howard, the contest judge, as a winner of the Pablo Neruda Poetry Prize and was published in the 1984 Fall/Winter edition of *Nimrod* literary review.

Dogs at the Concert

in an earlier version appeared in the 1996 anthology *Dog Music*.

Vows; Brass Tacks; and *Fields of Sense*

were part of a batch of poems awarded first place by William Stafford in a Western Washington University writing contest.

Tornado, 1953; and *On the Checklist of Saint Thomas Aquinas*

appeared in the Poetry Society of Michigan contest edition, Fall 2023.

Introduction

Poetry is language at play. In *New Songs of Innocence* S.J. Hodson is hard at work in this playground teasing us with syllabic verse ("Beside Himself with Calm"), haiku stanzas ("A Cougar Strolled By"), sonnet, ("Sonnet for Miriam"), and villanelle ("A Poet's Dark Night of the Soul"). He relishes the natural rhythm of speech and knows how to polish it metrically. He rhymes in wonderfully complex ways, combining end rhyme, internal rhyme, slant rhyme, sight rhyme and the unexpected sudden break from rhyme. Sentences unfold so nimbly as to seem utterly natural—just right, until Hodson makes one of them go just enough wrong to call their rightness to our attention and make us smile at what he has just done. We so delight in "So primed are we to see a face /We find them every anyplace." that we are a little startled to discover we have just finished a cleverly skewed villanelle. We would be in wonder at the depth of Hodson's knowledge of poetic form were we meant to notice it. But we aren't. And we don't. Until we do, and then our delight is doubled.

But poetry isn't just play, however clever. Language is a serious matter. It's not working unless it opens us up to our world. Beauty is at once at odds with and requires truth. In this ancient quarrel between poetry and philosophy, S.J. Hodson comes down squarely on both sides. The serious and the playful are for him sisters. His poetry has a habit of moving effortlessly back and forth—frequently within one poem—between everyday experience and philosophical reflection. One summer in Flint, Michigan "The air threw refrigerators / Up there with the birds/ . . . /appliances the air / Got tired of after only several miles." Meanwhile a family takes cover in their basement dining on "wilting saltines with Kool-Aid / And Baby Ruth candy bars / As tough as jerky – I've never liked them / Any other way since . . . . " In "Tornado, 1953," this childhood memory is paired with a reflection on life aboard an aircraft carrier to teach us what it means that wind does not blow the air around, but rather that wind is "an elastic mineral"

> . . . throwing itself around,
> And that the air is not particular.
> It disports itself with a largesse
> Not to be bought off — it will finesse
> Anyone's bomber.

At its best poetry teaches without preaching. If Blake's *Songs of Innocence* calls established religion into question to recover wonder at the religious spirit that gives birth to it, Hodson's *New Songs of Innocence* means to call into question science, the established religion of our time, to wonder again at what gives birth to it, the scientific spirit. *New Songs of Innocence* divides into an Overture and a Libretto. The Libretto in turn divides into sections on animal, mineral and vegetal, and then concludes by taking up musically what has been all the while musically taking these three worlds in—the personal. The title gives us still more. Songs of innocence must be new, fresh, young—not jaded by self-reflection. New songs of innocence presumably give us anew the new, fresh and young. This is a perennial necessity, for even innocence grows old. It is the work of the poets to renew it, showing us again the playful in the serious and the serious in the playful.

Stanley Hodson and I first met over fifty years ago as undergraduates. Neither of us quite fit. He was the son of evangelical Christians, I of lapsed communists. We studied Plato together. He introduced me to Wallace Stevens and Lightnin' Hopkins, and showed me why I had to understand Wittgenstein. He threw himself with inexhaustible gusto into academic study: literature, philosophy, anthropology, music theory—whatever enhanced his understanding of our being in the world. But he also performed at a coffee house called The Unmuzzled Ox, where he sang, played a mean blues guitar, and teased his audience with charm. For Hodson performance was always a version of teaching. To hear him play in song was to be enticed to see what you had always missed, indeed to see what could never be seen without first having been missed.

Then there was the Vietnam War. Hodson enlisted in the Navy and served a tour of duty on an aircraft carrier in the South China Sea. Once back home, unsure what to do, he experimented. A master's degree in philosophy, a series of quirky jobs—bell hop, apple picker, railroad boxcar painter, installer of heating and cooling systems . . . . Wherever he landed he soaked up the world's curious details, storing them in his remarkable memory, finding comparisons no one else would think of. Then he thought, perhaps he'd take a job as a college instructor, but no, that didn't quite fit his all-consuming style of learning. But a master's degree in creative writing and literature, yes, that might be at least a good place to pause and catch his breath. Hodson studied with Annie Dillard and completed his thesis, a collection of poems called *Beside Ourselves With Calm*. In 1984, a long poem from that collection, "Movement in a Solid—a Composite Figure of the Poet in the 20th Century" (included in this volume) was awarded a Pablo Neruda Prize in Poetry by *Nimrod* literary journal. Then practical life intervened, and Hodson worked for over a decade as the primary technical writer and editor for an industrial safety consulting firm where he wrote three books for that company. When his soul eventually and inevitably itched for something new, he went to law school at night, passed the bar, and practiced class-action labor law for almost twenty years, helping to recover millions of dollars in back wages for working people. When he retired in 2019, he began thinking exclusively (well, almost—he also formed a rock 'n' roll band) about writing—poetry naturally, but also a long-planned project rethinking biology, and science generally, in a way less subordinate to physics.

As a poet, S.J. Hodson is not really at home in our skeptical, subjective age. His poems probe our world deeply. They question, and so each brings to life the hope of answers.

Above the page there is something stirring,
A reach improvises the gravity
Where the mobile of words hangs true,
Is the sky where a poem can be a wing.

Writing poetry has been for Hodson like performing at The Unmuzzled Ox. He writes not so much to please his audience as to tease and teach his audience—and what a pleasure it is to be taught this way. Making poetry is for him serious—a way to think, a way to wonder. But he is also masterful at playfully seducing others to wonder. If "philosophy begins in wonder," these poems are invitations to philosophize. S.J. Hodson is one of the most interesting and talented poets of his generation, and yet he remains known to only a very few. In *New Songs of Innocence,* we are graced with his first published book of poetry. We should be thankful and hope it will not be his last.

OVERTURE

=/=/=/=

If Plants Were Just Chemicals

for Rod Burton

If plants were just chemicals
we'd eat dirt.

If animals were plants
we'd pet radishes.

If people were just animals
we'd marry kangaroos.

If angels were people
we'd pray to politicians.

We don't.

They aren't.

Movement In a Solid

A Composite Figure of the Poet in the Twentieth Century

for M. H. Abrams

1.

He put the gift of cut chrysanthemums
in a low, white bowl on the table prepared
against a windowful of autumn's depredations.

At the mirror his aging wife brushed her hair.
Her arm stroked and stroked in the dusk in the windowed
room, the movement a chant in a solid of evening air

In the wooden house in the woods in the hill side.
Her inner arm, the inner leg, relit still
by their own reflected light. The leg, reverberant

Down its solid length, like a spawning salmon
so shot with acids of longing in the blood
its flesh goes to ruin, worked and stroked

By the stream — itself only there while vanishing.
And nothing new in this, he knew. Presence: the threshold
where all things blur in the steady jostle

Of arriving departure — of departing arrival.
He early left occult auras all to others
and made his own this one blur only, bothered

By Sunday School images of angels on Jacob's
ladder, and his ruined thigh out of the socket.
All floating down on the left and up on the right,

Like good manners and an escalator at Sears
and Roebuck. He knew that — being angels —
they both came and went at once, like every thing else

In the solid of God's thought: old stones constant
on their way to sod, trees to wood, the sun
to light, and bodies to their secret bone.

2.

He had often felt that place in the woods nearby,
beside the garden walled against the deer,
where alders stood stepped within a massive

House long vanished down to its stones. Burned
utterly away and the ground long since
cleansed of ash, and only ghost violence

Left — the careful footings clubbed with moss
and their precincts all unfenced to trees mutely
ranged up through the stories of the place worse

Than moth or rust or thief, flaunting their littered
deep unfeeling of obliteration through
the Sunday pancakes, the cradle, the coupled bed,

The front room with its coffin. The alder house,
a dislocation of his heart he couldn't wrestle
right. And no help from prosperous historians

Or scientists, the bareness of their imaginations
fit only for realtors or such. As though the heavens
were a warehouse, and a forest came and went

Like the 5:19 to Dubuque. The vivid
solid of air standing down into his garden —
where the yearly companionate plants were fervid

In the light — was not for hire. On his earth
it was the ground that moved, the steady drift
of gravestones from their intended, beyond healing,

Old houses lifting their stepped roofs against
a wave so slow it could only be a feeling,
and his only calling to feel it, unfenced.

Youth

3.

As a youth he robustly strode the deck
of the apparent world, happy with the ocean's
game of solitaire, the taste of his own saliva,

Simple sleep, the pink of his fingernails,
and of course the attentions of handsome women.
But he listened with one ear to the Western gurus

Of undeception, people who cannot simply play
ball but who must go to bat, steal second,
and slide home in quantum mechanical cleats.

He sat in on their games glad to open the bidding
by throwing overboard his tribal maps and calendars.
But they saw him and raised him, and in a trice

Overboard and utterly went ship, sea, sky, and self.
Provincial they said, to think that we are something
Earth is wont to do. He caught the cold they said

Was the only mark of distinction left, and fell
to dissecting monotony. The quotidian beset
him; so he sang it, dry and sour in the mouth.

The ocean howled nonsense, sleep was work,
and, more and more willing to be alone, he forgot
the cocks that crow us up and the kinship

Of crickets in the grass was dust. The steady growth
of his unwilled body became an insult, another
catch of predatory autumn. *Death is the mother*

Of beauty, he said beautifully, *and the moon,*
of pathos and pity. All the while his wife
would not touch nor speak nor even write.

4.

The sky turned flat with deceit and hurt him.
Or maybe the tone of the sky was an echo
echoing the muteness of earth's pangs and poverties?

But in the poverty out of which we inherit
we are bounden to live as though deaf to the muteness?
And if radical unease is our element, he reasoned,

Then splendid disease is our highest deed.
So he practiced the ruined voice that he would need:
I sleep to wake and take what I can steal —

My youth was just a bad excuse for health.
Bruised stone and bone bruises never heal.
In desert dream, a stone bruise at my heel,

And that stone in my mouth my only wealth,
I sleep to wake and take what I can steal.
Hurtful words and old, words of woe and weal,

Murder my head and move my heart to stealth —
Bruised stone and bone bruises never heal.
My neck's a millstone, my shoulder is the wheel,

And sand is fit enough to drink my health;
I sleep to wake and take what I can steal.
My breast was beaten gold, my nerve was steel,

My love was splendid, cold, syphilitic wealth.
Bruised stone and bone bruises never heal.
Steel and stone, sand, gold, a shattered heel,

Health to ruin and goodwill gone to stealth,
I sleep to wake and take what I can steal —
Bruised stone and bone bruises never heal.

Grey Years

5.

With never any kisses to stun him peaceful
a lacquered loquacity took his mouth
for singing the shifty yes-and-no release

Of re-imagining rich the world imagined bare :
as though physics were wisdom and not just someone's
career : as if we were crystals with delusions

Of softness : as if when we looked into a face, dust
stared at dust : as though there were insects in insect
collections : as if when we pissed the urine just

Changed place : as if our parents' bodies were not
zones of fate : as if a corpse were just a piece
of damaged freight : as if hearkening and sight

And touch were not engines of the world but
just some shoddy practical joke the body
played on itself : as if we spoke rhapsodies

Of bleeps and squonks and spizzles utterly
senseless but for our fever to manufacture sense :
as though but for our domestications the sun's

Free animals of shadow, shape, and growth were brute
and brutal. This bareness became his credo once
he felt his life entered in the zero suited

To his clime. The suasion deepened. Reality itself
came to seem a fiction of some most november
imagination. He capitalized, apostrophized, apotheosized

Imagination. And from his muse he took lessons
on the tin can. For years he was hard at this.
Years he showed to the door of dust with never any kiss.

6.

Years went by. His mistress came too seldom,
and even when she did the ecstasy ran thin.
When one's most naked love may still be fake

What is there left to do but impotence?
He tried that for a while but it didn't take
his fancy. An inveterate, rustic frankness

Made him stop and take stock — he was lonely.
Formerly a brilliant fabulist, he remembered
the argument of a thousand fables: transcendence

Abandons him who sells it. And had he trundled
his angel to market? Yes. In poems and essays
too carefully sent round. His heart cleared

And everywhere he heard the pitch of dealers
in divinity, a yammering crowd hawking maps
with X's showing right where It was at. Composers

Sang that It was composition. Dancers,
affective-kinesthetic synaesthesia. Painters,
the inner eye. And then there were the scientists,

Their booths all along the thoroughfares: card tricks,
shell games, and button button who's got the button.
He felt some heartsickness for avid youth — with only blind

Alleys to choose from — and a little for himself,
having lost his song. He wasn't going anywhere,
he felt; but then, he wasn't going wrong.

He'd begun to guess that perhaps no love less
naked than the Earth could truly please.
He was sick of even splendid disease.

Home

7.

He began to sleep well, and to like his anonymity,
did the shopping and the laundry with his wife,
often walked the grounds of a nearby university

Prosperous for its fisheries and forestry departments.
One day one fall he went to watch the college salmon
spawn, to see them after their several years' abandon

In the freedom of ocean climb the pouring ladders
they had descended in their youth and make their homecoming
in the basin by the yacht club. The shallow pool

Stirred with animals solid as his thigh,
stroking and breathing the autumn water, trusting
their naked eyes to it. He joined the crowd on the bank.

Boisterous young men and women from Fisheries caught
the salmon barehanded. Male and female sorted
they them. And the audience applauded,

Thinking the fish would go then to some breeding ground
to lift the mating dance and sow the stream
with young. But out came knives and cleavers.

The pregnant bellies were slit open over buckets.
Dead males were flexed into the eggs. And a hand-slosh
to finish the job. Into the sudden quiet

One of the fish girls shrugged and said, "They'd die
anyway." The witnesses went their separating ways,
heads down, shoulders hunched. Some days later his shoulders

Loosened and he saw his way clear into the language:
dying anyway is what all living beings do
but they never die just any way if they can help it.

8.

He sat of an evening and watched the light out
of the world, watched his wife brush the secret
oils of her body out and out into her hair. He sat

And did his kind of grooming, sloughing dead images
of death: not the mother of beauty nor the assassin
waiting at the ladder, but the brother — and the twin

Identical — of human life and truth as troth.
Eyes and lips, belly, breast, and thigh that couldn't die
would be pumice, or shellac. This strange body they both

Were, where bruises came and went like slow clouds
in a solid air. The trouble with life was not
abandonment, the trouble was a god everywhere

Too near. Did the fishes — who were muscled water — know
that there was ocean? He leaned into the storm
of silence at the frame of the world, a storm become

More his intimate than those of light and air.
And he settled to his art from above — the old fevers
to make, or at the least to find, just the lighting

Of so many candles in the sun. As though there weren't
enough light abroad in the day. Simple flowers
were candles enough — their bodies flames of scent.

Berries ripened in the forest. Inside its stone walls
the garden rose and fell. On the floor of the ruined
orchard at the alder house the deer ate apples

Sweetened with bruises. And he kept cut flowers
in a low, white bowl on a table prepared
against a windowful of autumn's depredations.

Vows

Spring, when the cats stop eating from tins,
Sleeping on beds. When the birds skim in
Unsubsidized. Living a tree at a time,
Owning no maps, keeping no calendars.

Not checking in with customs, the animals —
Whose each life is the first — are driven
There in the middle of our world, a stake
To ground us. Taking us down

To the trees, whose vow is even purer.
Ranged cumberously up thin light and air —
Owning no feet, keeping no eyes —
Each year trees live the very first year,

Or farthest down into stone, the bed —
The gong going down into the first minute.

LIBRETTO

=/=/=/=

Animal

= / = / =

What the Air is to the Birds

Not quite as thick as
The water is to us, but
Thicker than the air.

Like skiers in snow,
They're slaloming as they come,
Smearing arcs and stops.

Does this mean compared
To minnows, water to whales
Is plashy as air?

And compared to us,
What is air to elephants,
Snorting its ether?

I've seen porpoises
Race the sea — without batting
A muscle, their sheath

Of skin, one entire
Unending peristaltic
Ripple, swallowed by

Ocean like earthworm
Swallowed by Earth, like the birds
Gulped up by the Air.

Dogs at the Concert

Sometimes we're at life
the same way dogs are
at a concert.

We hear all the sounds
and none of the music.

Sown with Next Spring, Last Spring

for Michael and Susan Davis

Each spring the pond breathes out — dragonflies.
Who mate and die — the pond breathes in.
Sown with next spring last spring.
A courtship flight and stir of dragonflies
Was underway on the pond's face

Sunday, two kinds kissing kind
For kind's sake. As wrens to robins in their size
And pertness, the small ones blue and blue-greened,
The large ones only powder blue. Tomorrow lies
Over some threshold for the small ones

Coupling on the wing, almost as fleet conjoined
As they were single. But the powder-blues
Are a different thought, and for three more days
They don't mate and they don't wait.
Something that isn't time goes by

For them — the season of the heartbeat
And hand- and toe-nail — as sunk as frogs in mud
In themselves. And is it that it slows,
Or does it widen, for the sumac, rose,
And moss?

Beside Himself with Calm

Beside himself with calm one
Day, Rilke stood in
A zoo in France. The world played over

His features, arranging his
Face and shoulders with
Things he met. There were flamingos there —

Wherever a zoo in France
Is for flamingos.
Their breast feathers showed where a breeze was

Going. The birds slept — what kind
Of dream comes down to
Drink at flamingo heads? He stood by

The birds like resolutions
Made for him by friends.
They all woke there…somewhere — Rilke had

Forgotten. They stretched — he felt
His coat bind. They turned
And strode, out of France, along the earth.

The Cicada Test

At least the desert people know the locust
Is meat. When the cicadas throb
Their seventeen-year orgasm, climbing
From the earth and tree roots like a zombie
Movie in a cohort of generation

Bedecking every tree trunk, porch railing,
And sandbox bench with their blown-glass
Skeletons, if you're five years old
And you still have eyes to see and ears
To hear, you know your yard has mysteries

Of fellowship older than the ground,
Singing three days and nights of insect
Copulation, sowing the soil
With another seventeen-year sleep.
When you're twenty-five and trying to breathe

In a graduate hive where the greybeards
Say they love wisdom, if they do not evince
Even one wince of grok about the weird
Of life and sensation at the Earth's breast —
If they cannot pass the cicada test,

Then you know to shake the dust
Of that cavern off your sandals
And get on down the road.

Deer Saliva

On the manhole cover in the clover
Alley I pour seed from the feed store
For the squirrels, towhees, and rabbits.

This morning a six-point buck snuck
Into the buffet, prehensile tongue lapping away
At the food platter, in no mood

To share with the mere four-point youngster
Trying to get close, darting his nose past the elder's
Stamping front left hoof, a blunt gesture

Pounding the seed to flour, conking little brother
On the head, a last kick daubing his side
With seed dust smear. Dominance made clear,

The younger is glad of blackberry leaf salad,
And they step onward, no hard feelings.
The squirrels come gleaning just after, like hyenas

In the tough wake of lions. There's seed enough
For them in the embossed metal, and they've lost
None of their appetite, in no way put off

By the deer saliva sauce.

Likenings

The jay and the towhee
Bounce through the branches
Of the willow like the ball
Bearings in the pinball machine.
One-fifth their size, the finches

Seethe the willow canopy
Like sand fleas in seaweed.
The flicker, gaudy lord of this wood,
Enters the bouffant of the leaves
Like the barrette on the beauty queen.

A Triad in the Key of Urgent

The doe is not saying to herself *...and then...*
and then...and then... She's not
Saying *...maybe...maybe...* With no certain

Good to draw her near, no certain ill
To flee, she just stands until
Her surround bespeaks her,

Head cocked to the thrum
Of her autism spectrum.
The deer, squirrel, rabbit, bird

Are like singers stunned by song
And pouring it along; like dancers who live
That movement where even rest is a hive

Of stir, never paused, always gadding.
They have prows but no faces, no cladding.
They're loops of looping just like our viscera,

Topped out at three chakras: groin, belly, and lung —
Mating, eating, and the play of fellow feeling.
Deer, rabbit, squirrel, bird,

Each one a chord poured
In the key of fervid.

Driving with Bees

for Anita Boyle and Jim Bertolino

So there they were with a live hive
In the back of their Subaru,
Tooling down Guide Meridian
Road in the cool of the morning
With the car a/c set on cool —

To keep the bees somnolent.
And doing a wary drive,
Deliberate — almost grave —
Circling the roundabouts, careful
Of insulting the inertial

Sense of the hive — as who should want
Nauseous bees in the back seat?
Something of a perfect koan
for a poet couple and a couple
Of poets: if you want the meat,

It will cost blood; and if honey,
You may have to be supple
Through the sting. A hive is an ancient,
Alien thing. Crustacean,
Antennaed, exo-skeletal,

And furred. And nausea is all
To the point: because honey
Is bee regurgitant.

A Cougar Strolled By

haiku stanzas

Three days ago on
  September first, a cougar
walked casually

Through my yard in full
  daylight and into the woods
below and behind

My home by the trail
  I cut in the bramble for
the deer — the cat was

Probably scenting
  the deer who were here the night
before on that trail.

It was 8:00 a.m.
  for the lazed cougar saunter,
body the size and

Color of a brown
  Labrador, but with a head
that means business — that's

Okay by me, mine
  means business, too. And so I
strolled down my trail and

Peed on the threshold
  in the woods — scent markers are
oratorios

For cougars and deer.
  And of course I'm hoping that
my piss doesn't smell

Like beef *au jus*
  to a cougar.

Wearing a World

In the gap you cut in the blackberry
Bramble, do you see the doe
Sampling the morning sounds? You know

How that gap feels to you, the hours
It took your handedness to crop
And mince and clear it, the strop

Of thorns catching at your pant legs,
The plashy spill of the willow
When the wind tips the rainy pours

Of leaves. For you it's a place out of doors
But she has never lived with doors,
Either in or out. Her two doorless children

Stand by, still, waiting for a sign
From her to move. She is breathed
By the woods, and her fawns are breathed

Of her. She is a brown motif
In the sonata of green —
Her skin ends exactly where the seam

Of forest, her overcoat, closes.

Arcs of Ripe

The head-butt tree, a willow,
Is healing its antler-
Scored body a layer

Of layered fiber per year
For two extruded years now,
A slow way to go

But its only way is slow.
Years I sought and bought
For it in the black wire

Roll of fencing I coiled
It in. The rut scent oiled
Into it by the buck insistent

On scraping off his bloody velvet
Fades. But still each doe
Who passes in her estrous,

Even the lame sister who dare
Not mate, flinches at the raw
Tree, then, skittish, nears

The beaconing lust magnet
To sideways sip the perfume scent
Pregnant with all future deer.

Swallowed in the Shell

The doe came up out of the snow-drowned
Woods, and following her long-headed nose found
The peanuts I had scattered for the jays,

Even though covered, buried, frozen.
I went down to my sliding glass door
To stalk her, to let the food cozen

Her into bent stillness for her photograph,
Moving slowly only when she dropped her eyes
To eat, pausing for each startled head rise

Until she, calmed, returned to scouring
Up the ground nuts, shell and all.
Then she smelled under the snow fall

The bird seed spilled from the feeder, not roasted
Like the peanuts but oily in their minute fatness,
Licking them up by scent in their frosted

Snow gravy. Then back she went, dissolving
Into woods, swallowed whole in her shell
Of sight and fur and smell.

Nested

July 6, first fawn sighting,
Ox-eyed, knock-kneed, maybe five
Weeks old, springing up the weed
Bank behind the sedately
Matron doe. Cold, wet, late Spring —
All trees at least one month more
Dormant than last year, green world
Somnolent, pent, pregnant leaved.

Pregnant does ruminant in
Paused gestation? Curled in beds
Of bracken, slowing the throb
Clock of uterus? Kiln chocked
Fractally with eyes and knees
And next uterus.

Mineral

= / = / =

Dust and Juice

after Rob Frost

Some say the world is born of dust,
Some say of juice.
I don't see the use of betting,
Most eggs I've met
Are both. But if I must
I guess I go with wet.
For as the story has it,
Though we're both earth
And spit, the spit is God's —
Pretty good odds
That juice is first.

Brass Tacks

The porcelain in the sink,
    from the bed of which river?

The metals in the faucet,
    from the seams of which mountain?

The leather in the shoes,
    from the skin of which body?

The wood in the table,
    from the stand of which forest
    in what light under which clouds
    on what soil….?

The sink, faucet, shoe, table…,
    from the well of whose life on what day?

Tornado, 1953

When I was a kid I thought the wind blew
The air around. Then war came, and the President
And both Houses of Congress sent me
To the naval air wing, where they knew
That wind is air throwing itself around,
And that the air is not particular.
It disports itself with a largesse
Not to be bought off — it will finesse
Anyone's bomber.

Air: an elastic mineral. Absorbent,
Soaking up each needle on each spruce
That ever will be, each grain of lifted salt, grit.
And it takes our hearts to itself,
Sponsoring in us from day-one
A compulsive interest in the invisible.

Even some people who have been there
Say there are mountains and plains
On the moon. But those are metaphors.
How can there be mountains meant
Where there's no wind to groom them?
And stand on them miles deep, beneficent
Enough for a world.

One Michigan summer in Flint
The air threw refrigerators
Up there with the birds.
We moved into the basement,
Ate wilting saltines with Kool-Aid
And Baby Ruth candy bars

As tough as jerky — I've never liked them
Any other way since, mislaid
From my father's store delivery job.
That summer Dad was an agent
Of Metropolitan Insurance, and he paid
For truckloads of appliances the air
Got tired of after only several miles.

Singing Through Three Zip Codes

Singing through three zip codes in its bed
To the Bay, the utterance of my neighborhood creek
Is born on Samish Ridge, a schizophrenic

Hill equal parts Mirkwood and Faerie glade,
The two creek strands folding like cake batter just
Before they dive under the path, lading on

As one ululating syllable with
Glottal stops. The forest says its pithy
Moan only when the wind combs it the wrong way

But the hillside is a constant Tourette
Syndrome of muttered water, chanting through
Whenever the freeway susurrus mutes

With night. The creek expresses ground water
From under rec rooms, sick rooms, barbecues,
And deadfalls, moss walls, holly, alder, and fir.

The creek and its sibling creeks threading
Down the bowl of the hills keep their mud-brown
Bottoms until the last moment and the thrawn,

Quirked leap just under the bridge, the pont,
Of DuPont Street beside the Bay, where, wanting
To save the bridge and post office from washing away,

The city sleeved the rapids with concrete
Into a widened, banked estuary — which seals
Swim up into, their noses wrinkling the genteel

Surface of the tamed water, savoring the taste
Of the kiss of this mouth of the hills
With its redolence of forest.

On the Checklist of Saint Thomas Aquinas

On the checklist of
  Saint Thomas Aquinas, the
Earth qualifies as

An angel, flexed and
  embodying opposites:
all times of night and

Day present somewhere
  always, all seasons urgent
always, winter on

Mountain tops, desert
  summer whispering thousands
of dead miles to sand.

Knowing by species
  only, incapable of
even seeing an

Individual —
  the whale, elephant, even
less than a spider

Crumble drift in the
  doorway of Earth's mansion of
the quartering Moon.

A Stun

Light enters the wood as a seep,
The way blood enters a scrape,
And the heaped dark unveils as scape
And lay, and exhalation of shape.

The animals are an ooze
Of ground split off in twos
Of trance and mating dance whose
Pivot is to bruise, fuse, drowse.

The trees beat slow as ocean
Fronds of seaweed in stirred motion
Turning light into a devotion
Of green sap, lignin, resin.

The people build and nest and house,
And turn the forest into vows
And promises of art, and rouse
To curate the beat of ebbs and flows.

Light stands into the wood in a pour
As thick as fur, corduroy, velour,
And shows the wood is not a floor
But a stun of caught sun.

Michael Faraday was a Sandemanian

Michael Faraday
  was a Sandemanian
who took inductance

For angelic presence,
  and who's to say he was wrong? —
invisible song

Of sleight resonance
  in coiled wire, rocking in locked
slinky spills tickling

Like a vorpal blade,
  vrooming like a light-saber,
timeless as a star.

Michael waned young, and
  then he waxed incandescent
in fame, and flourished —

The prime minister
  asked him the worth of angel
electricity,

And Faraday shot
  him a grin and said, *Someday*
you'll see, you'll tax it.

Military Airframes

for Emily Dickinson

None of them is beautiful except
In the manner of a horseshoe crab.
They're all exoskeleton, skid, sled.

They're projectiles extorting lift.
Without blowtorch thrust they're as airworthy
As a manhole cover.

They are to wave as board,
To meadow as pavement,
To air as axe.

Their muscles are hydraulic;
Their nerves, electronic;
Their song, trans-sonic.

They're winged howitzers,
Never clean except as a lizard is —
Oil dusted, dry-licked, eyes a hooded radar tic.

Vegetal

= / = / =

Harrowed Into New Root

A cedar stump two feet across is the fern
And fungus buffet in the back corner
Where the woods lap the lawn,
With a ghost tree ninety feet shy
Socketing the stump in the mind's eye.

A seven-year-old cherry and an infant
Maple have rooted in the stump, taking
It for ground in their wrest and want,
The now generation serenely ignorant
Of the thrust in the buried surround.

The blackberry bramble in a smother
Of gossip stitching the woods edge,
The thorned canes a Velcro-ratcheted hedge
The deer tunnel through unbothered,
Their fur dense and sleek, forest otters.

The stump cooks open like roast meat
In its annual rings, the slow oven
Of green fire unweaving its fabric
Into soil, the banked sunlight
Harrowed into new root.

The Tree Man

The arborist, the forester, the steward
Of trees came to see my liquidambar,
Eight feet of its trunk shattered

Off by the wind from the freeway corridor.
Just light enough for me to shoulder
The carcass downhill to my driveway, where

I dismembered its thirteen year-old body.
I asked for sawed dressing of the ragged stump
And pruning of the branches for the clumped

New center of gravity and torsion of the tree.
And since I didn't need haulage of debris,
The arborist just went straight up the torso

With a curved sickle of handsaw and a chain saw
Hanging from his belt, leaned back in his harness
Like a telephone lineman. With unerring finesse

Of amputation, he balances the mobile
Of limbs hanging from the tree's head and mouth
In the ground up into the air. He speaks of growth

Hormones and of the tree's desires,
Making it obliquely clear he knows
That trees are visitant in the land,

With their own urgencies not to be denied,
Mislaid, parlayed. Trees are a phage
Going where they want to go. His leverage

Is to humor them, stroke them, nudge
Them — a tree whisperer, farrier, therapist.
For most things we tend, we're drudges

And slowpokes: horses, dogs, radios,
Internal combustion engines, bridges,
Cell phone towers. But compared to trees

We have faerie quickness, revving at pell-mell
Beats per tree-reflex. When one of us merges
With a tree, that's Zen work, courted trance, angel

Rhythm, slowing down enough to catch
Up with them, quieting to match their pitch —
Pruning in 40 minutes what the tree hears

To grow into for forty years.

The Woods Are Where the Earth Breaks Open

The woods are where the Earth breaks open into almost
Faces, a parliament of leaves, of eyes and tastes
Applauding light, a susurrus and a sough of flight

Harboring in trees. To be present with nature naturing,
The framers of our human parliament were De-ists
Separating church and state, ushering priests

Firmly to the sidelines of war and peace. The wood
Is where the Earth breaks open — churches are too
Closed and fervent for our own good.

The woods are where the deer and the cougar flare,
The hawk and the hare, and in their worship, stare
Straight through us, offering a compliment

We can rise to, and mostly won't.

Fire / Wood

for Tom Sherwood

Fire is wood making off with itself.

The wood breaks open its store
Of flame, spends itself gone.

Wood is fire making room for itself.

The wood awakes from its solid dream,
Flame raises its head — they leave together.

Fire burns down as wood burns up.

Wood is light being a tree.
Till something gives
In the wood — the fire gets out.

The wood strains...misses.
Holds a moment...slips.
Finally catches, on fire.

Farmer's Pride

My mother, Virginia May,
Told me out of the blue one day
What her father once told her
Down in their orchard
Behind the kitchen garden

In Haverhill, Kansas, 1934.
Leaning on the fence built
To keep the cow's milk
From tasting like cider,
His overalls dung-smeared,

His left thumbnail blue-black
From a badly swung hammer —
And she, petulant, she said,
And young, and weary
Of being a farm girl:

> *Just consider that all*
> *Of civilization, each skyscraper,*
> *The highways, banks, the navy,*
>
> *Ice cream parlors and movie*
> *Theaters, come out of*
> *Three inches of topsoil.*

Sometimes in Some Winds

Sometimes in some winds
You can tell which tree in the wood
Is the tongue of which cry
Of air, but mostly the wood
Is one swollen throat, one long
Slow-pulled scab of sigh.

The Wood Stands In Itself

The wood stands in itself,
A held breath, cupped pool, brimmed berry,
Each cone shot through with unborn trees,

Cocked, waiting for the sun burst
Still struggling its way from the contortionist
Body of the star — standing in itself,

A whipped cauldron, smashed pumpkin
Feed-mash, star-pulp, each spume
Shot with unborn forest.

The Glade that Was

When we find our way
by a stand of trees,
in the sway of their bodies
we can feel a promised house.

When we live clothed
by a wooden house,
we can feel the glade
that was.

Personal

= / = / =

French Intensive Weeding

My old-age, hillside home is dug
Into the drinking throat of a bay
So compellingly facing heaven
I have to look away
To run an errand.

Many sins ago I lived some blocks
From here, an enlisted sailor in a fug
Of war. My war bride was a grad student
Science girl who showed me her pressed plant
Collection and taught me there's a local tree
Whose Botany true name is False Hemlock —
Which seemed like bad science and good poetry.

That war is so gone it's not even movies now.
I maunder over the weeding of my rain-drain
Gravel steps, refusing to spill poison
Into the ground water, making it a meditation
Of inverse French Intensive Gardening,
Gloves off, carefully pulling the complete root
Systems like coaxing the guts from a slit fish,
Piling the immediately limp, minute
Lives for the toss into the woods bracken.

Arms

When you put your mind
To that kind of work
Dropping napalm on folk,
It changes your gait,
Gives you a deathly hand

Lying in wait there, shading
The kiss, the deal, the allemande
Left. No one else sees it, sly
Dog in the weeds, biding.
That hand — like the portrait

Of Dorian Gray — deeps its sins
In secret. It can take decades
To slough its burnt skins

And rejoin the body.

A Rainbow Is An Embed

A rainbow is an embed, not an appliqué —
We're fools for eye-hand co-ordination,
But the biosphere's no engineer, it's a musician

Of riffs and licks and sips of organ-ized play.
The horizon is a line we have to walk to guide on —
All birds are born with lift they have to learn to ply,

Legs are limber bones that have to walk to harden,
All kids are mouthed with phonemes they have to learn to say.
Whatever riot Eden was, it was not a garden.

A rainbow is an embed, not an appliqué,
Leeching all its colors from the place it's found in,
Derivative, a parasite, gristle in light's way.

Ears are born for fright and flight, drinking the surround in
Front/back and left/right nearings of dismay —
But they can exfoliate harmonies of unison.

We're thrown as fools of eye-hand coordination,
We're tools of ourselves and deep confounded.
The rainbow is an embed, not an appliqué,
And there we are, gristle in the sway.

Sleeping Under Cloth

Ecclesiastes 4:11

Our friends are on the road, late-life beloveds
Sleeping under cloth in this year of late spring
And chill summer. They email a photo
Of their tent — across the lake, just above
The pine tree in the foreground. *For when two*

Lie down together, they shall keep warm.
Their cloth house barely holding their breath
Around them as they curl, spooning, in airs
From the Arctic and off the ocean, the stars
Like a bell jar over them, bending frozen

Liquid light on their dear persons, kissing
Their folding bedroom ceiling with the blessing
Of being beloveds who found themselves.

Choirs of Done

The patient siding on the old house,
Enclosing our sleep, our wake,
Applied a careful strake at a time,

Leveled, notched, fastened by hand
By someone somewhere in the ground.
These are ghosts, their actual stir,

Each made-structure a blur
Of past doing and choice.
The built-surround a choir

Of hand print and eye squint.

The Ojai Valley

Just home from the Vietnam War and doing penance
For dropping napalm on people, trying to stop
Himself doing more harm, he was a bellhop
For three years at The Inn where convalescents
Thirty years earlier had recouped

Themselves from war wounds, the resort
Where the Flying Tigers and their consorts
Still came annually to drink themselves to their knees.
The Tigers, a legendary World War II group
Only then just recently outed as the U.S. military's

Fighting force that masqueraded as being Chinese
Controlled. They drank right through the ambulance
Call for one of their own, collapsed on the bar terrace,
The stretcher bearers hustling across the putting green,
The party growing more antic, hectic, in the face

Of heart attack. One man had a kidney bypass
Bag which he casually emptied in the lavatory,
And then dived back into the camaraderie.
At the storied Inn the celebrity
Quotient was high. In his time there he waited on

Telly Savalas, Paul Newman and Joanne
Woodward, Burt Lancaster, and Raymond
Massey. When he took cans of beer to Newman,
He was reviewing the script that would become
The movie: *Fort Apache, The Bronx*. A fighting theme

Ran through the whole staff, half of whom
Were paperless immigrants, and some of the white men
Bristled at being lumped with them —
And around it all, the Valley stood
In colors like a choral ode to bedded

Stone as old as the air and waters.
Most of that workplace was out of doors.
In all seasons and weather, he made his rounds
In polished black dress shoes, slacks, cummerbund,
And bowtie, white dress shirt and green bolero jacket —

Toting wood and building fires in fireplaces,
Hauling ashes, and buckets of ice and six-packs
Of beer, and bags and bags and suitcases,
Lending a permanent crick to his spine.
Living daily with the mountains of the Los

Padres Forest, faced with rock older than faces
And staring right at you if you had a mind
To see. Daily towered over by stone close
To a god, so lichened and slow that we're a mist,
A stop-action fog on the Valley floor, just

Spume among the waves of trees seething
Any ground they can on that rocky shore.
Wars, and even centuries, can fall away
There. Dying Flying Tigers can breathe
Their last on a putting green, and the sway

Of light around a cliff, a height, a peak,
Sets the measure where death is a tweak
Of life. Where a whole tide and surf of wear

Can go out and leave you just standing there —
For a beachcombing spirit-god to find you
And breathe on you and polish a facet or two.

43 Years After Vietnam Deployment

for Rick & Jan

They're older but they've still got juice,
Out early each summer morn
To take the measure of his garden,
Talking in that fluent loose
Unison an octave apart
Of man and woman long partnered.
Careful of heart, tending the horn
Of plenty so it doesn't harden
Before the grandkids are born.

She's the navigator on long drives,
Calling out each arcane turn
The route insists on. And she's in charge
Of the open-fire grill in the yard,
And of last things for her mom.

He's steady, wry, and musical.
For years a school principal,
He's become a volunteer judge,
And in the young men hauled hard
By the State, he and I see lives
That might have fallen to his dad and mine
If war hadn't shown them how to spend
Themselves for king or country.

Forty-three years ago, and counting,
He and I were shipmates in the long grudge
Of the Vietnam War. The years bend
All of that away. The sun wants to burgeon,

To stand down into the garden and get thick
In berry and leaf. The heart wants the large
Beat — summer — and the nifty lick
On the guitar, the curl and skirl
Of handmade old new music.

I don't do things by half, my Girl,
He answers her on what he has in hand.

The long haul takes nothing less than all.

Inventing a World to Love

for Dawn

When our families first met in the scraped-desert
Bulldozed orange-grove brand-new subdivision
World of Scottsdale, Arizona, Eisenhower
Was still in the White House, just. Everyone
Was from somewhere else, brought, hurtling,

By Ike's new bulldozed interstate highways.
No lawns, no flowers, no shade from the baby trees,
Just concrete and rock hard caliche soil,
The kind that earlier tribes made adobe of.
We kids were all inventing a world to love,

Like those we'd left over the horizon,
Earnest and working at it almost consciously
Because new friends, real ones, were an oasis
In the barren. And there was Dawn,
And her folks and her brother Richie —

And she, oh my goodness, was a quiet
Firecracker, with her mother Nina's wit
And tact, and luxuriant auburn hair pouring
From her head, such a gorgeous flourishing
Girl-head of hair. And she shone as a gymnast

In those early years of girls doing new things.
In time, she and my brother married and the babies
Came, and thank goodness for them —
Pushy importunate creatures but then
They turn into people we couldn't do
Without. There she was, a twelve-year-old omen
Of time-past, time-future, time now.

Eddie and Heather

The man has his first-born daughter
Riding astride his shoulder,
Her arm across his forehead, facing his ear,

Her other hand gripping the hair
At the back of his head. *Is she ready for the car?*
That's the question hanging on the air.

Nooo! she says a bit plaintively,
Gently kicking her heels at his chest and back,
Nooo, she says a bit heartbrokenly,

I want my pittow — that's how she says *pillow* —
As comfortable as any mahout on her elephant,
In charge as any drover on her special camel.

Smoke and Sadie Jo

for Leila

The man, married to my first sister,
And their first-born daughter
Are dancing to boogie rock and roll —

Father, leaning from the couch he's lying on,
Holding the tiny girl's hands above her head,
Her feet planted tight together, pointed

Just so in the pivot they're working
As he bobs and dips her, swooping and jerking
Her to the beat, her calm face turned

The whole while over her shoulder to me,
Huge solemn eyes saying, *You see,*
This is how it's done.

Epictetus Country Western Song

for Jack Day

Jim Lagos was a New Jersey merchant mariner,
Sleek as a seal, tough as a steel ball bearing,
Chuckle like a glass-pack muffler
Worn and tuned within an eyelash
To a down-shift, rippled gruff.

He'd had a first family, sown and grown
And lost in the years when he was mostly at sea,
And probably better that way for them,
He said, because he hadn't known
Then his good times when he was in them.

He was sailing into and out of San Francisco
Twenty years earlier in the Sixties,
And that's when he began to make art,
Abstract and jagged, etched on metals
With toxic chemicals in an industrial park.

He was doing big-time installations
For corporate clients, works hung on façade,
In HQ lobby, atrium, and boardroom,
But he was only halfway home and still off-stride
Because he didn't know good times when he was in them.

In my early forties when I first met him,
The chemicals he'd used had etched his liver,
But it didn't show and he didn't know
And in his sixties he felt young,
So he and his second family were purring along.

His new daughter was in my wife's second grade classroom;
She was shiny as a razor and plump as a grape.
She came in her pajamas and curled in his lap,
Her ear against his heart like a squirrel monkey possum,
And he said now he knew good times when he was in them.

He said that was his whole store of wisdom,
That he didn't need anything more anymore.
And that was good because he died soon after,

Leaving the echo of his rumbled laugh
Blessing himself for having lived in tandem
The good times he'd known while he was in them.

Drunks at a Port Orchard Wedding

He said yes, he'd be a groom's man,
Because he'd never been before,
Nor to Port Orchard, the bride's hometown.
Besides, whenever again would he get to dress
In a robin's egg blue Riverboat Gambler
Tuxedo? Ruffles at throat and wrist.

At the bride's folks' place afterward,
Avoiding an indoor reception he's under
The apple trees in the back yard,
Where it turns out young matrons are leaving
Their infants for the call of the party
Inside. They rotate the duty
Of minding the children, at first,
Then tacitly leave him to do it — checking on him
Less and less frequently, until it's just
The newborn in an abatement of time.

The children are quiet, mannerly, drunk on the drowse
Of June and shade and themselves.
He feels them work their marveled balance,
Each least movement immense, intensest trance.
The milk-blue sea rests away.
Mountains busy the horizon. A jay
Stirring the boughs of the apple trees
Is there just because he can be,
The same reason blue stirs along his body.
The sky stands right down on the babies'
Heads, constantly drops on them
Its silent tons. Their spittle is a clear

Sap the grasses take. Purple shadows come
And go in their eye and ear sockets —
Each more deeply jointed to the world
Than the set of leg or arm.

The newlyweds in her girlhood front room,
Hands drunk on gifts and mouths full of words that come
With handfuls of gifts. The chorus of bored
Young couples lounging, drunk on hard
Cider and ceremony. And out back
In the drinking grasses under the trees,
The evening drunk on the babies.

Sonnet for Miriam

It's early, and the moon still blows its horn
Of quiet light against the deepening blue
Of day. The children, and their mothers too,
Are perky with the hour. It's field-trip morn.
The second grade is bound away for miles
To the south. I'm here as Teacher's husband.
Just as my teacher's husband stood, we stand
This morning the kids and I, trading guarded smiles.

Then up skips Miriam, glowing soft as pearls —
When we first knew her, she wasn't even born!
She holds my hand in welcome, then she's gone
With her friends, quick minnow in a school of girls.
  What constellation is it where such moments shine?
  I don't know its name, I just know it's mine.

Remembering

Life holds a mystery from side
To side, from front to back and roof
To floor. It doesn't take much proof
To show that some men flinch and hide
From this at full stride.

As though life's only good on-task —
Unmixed with thoughtfulness in time,
And if in passing you say to them,
"Which is the fruit, and which the husk?"
Their answer is, "Don't ask."

Rafe Hart had a different way —
He could run and at the same time tarry.
Keeping his poise inside of hurry,
He'd check his thought, then grin and say
Something full and wry.

That's how he was when I saw him last
In deep July of '98.
The summer sun let down its weight
Of light, and he and I worked fast
Then went to shade to rest.

We had a lake, a live band for sound,
The birds were watchful in the trees.
The company's young families
Spread blankets all around
And poured their children on the ground.

Rafe and I sat, our duties done:
We'd shifted tables and umbrellas,
And sampled boiled shrimp, as well as
Ale. Watching the children,
He spoke of his daughters and son.

He started, as one does, with news
Of them: the latest job, travel, plan.
Then our talking paused, and we began
To ponder, to muse,
Thinking aloud in ebbs and flows.

We agreed there's no blessing so right
As to see young people well grown,
And that there is no gift so fine
As the gift they bring us straight
From untaught insight.

As Rafe warmed to our subject, he glowed
With quiet pleasure, and said his thanks
For his wife as partner and mother.
While all around us the party roared
With squirt-guns and pranks.

The Earth was beautiful that day,
Each leaf and blade of grass alive,
And each young family so brave.
The lake and the land had their say,
And the sky stood away.

By now we've seen this Earth from outer space,
Just floating there like a blue picnic
Beside a lake of stars and dark.
We're it, it's ours, and for us its face
Is a human face.

To lose a man like Rafe back to the Earth
Is to see and think the Earth anew.
There's nothing else to do
With such a mystery: He had breath!
...he was here!...there was birth....

Let this writing be a wreath
In honor of Rafe Hart.
He was a man who took his part
With gracious wit, and now the Earth
Receives him into memory.

Facings

So primed are we to see a face —
In leaf litter, clouds, or in the moon —
We find them everyplace.

Pareidolia's what they call this phase
Of ours. What it means is we're a loon,
So primed are we to see a face.

We pace the world from face to face,
Like Tarzan on his vines, like a baboon
From mate to mate. We find them everyplace.

We're so timed to run this race
We even face the clock, the dish and the spoon
That ran away together . . . . So primed are we for face.

The baby cannot talk or walk, so it gives face
As deep as life, and we fall into it as soon
As birth and sure as fate. It works anyplace.

The tiniest mark, the faintest trace,
On stone, in rune, it's enough to go on —
So primed are we to see a face
We find them every anyplace.

:•{
;^•\
§] :^)<
'•\
=/=

The Look of Love

Some say that love is just a one-night stand,
Some say a life-long grind, a burrow.

But in that moment, beauty-stunned
And by succulence of voice,

The look of love is both release
And tomorrow.

Bouncing Ball Song

after Tony Connor

William Yeats
had faerie beats
both wizened
and bedizened.

William Blake
was a flake
of the bleak
and sanest kind.

T.S. Eliot
was an un-hip cat
but he could
jam and jellicle.

Wallace Stevens
was at sixes and sevens,
but he could roar
with a bellyful of syllable.

Emily Dickinson
issued tickets on
the azure express
to dawn.

Walter Whitman
wrote himself to fit
as Walt, and Wit,
and Everyman.

Wystan Auden
said we oughtn't
leap without looking
but that leap, we must.

e.e. cummings
went typewriter drumming
and beat poems to a dust
of punctuation lost.

Robert Frost
was never lost —
two roads, at most,
diverging.

Theodore Roethke
made himself a breath key
to unlock wake-
and-sleep emerging.

Dylan Thomas
set his compass
by whiskey
and possession.

Tony Connor
was a goner
until Pegasus
rode *him* to a lather.

That Time

When the day is suspended
Like a bead of water skinned
Only with water at the tip
Of a leaf stem or tree bud's end,

With nothing turning
But the light dimming
From flare to glimmer,
And the air over and in

Everything bated only by air,
And the anyplace you stand
Is the every where.

A Poet's Dark Night of the Soul

for Tony Connor

He lost the pulse of poetry for a spell —
In a country of three hundred million,
Writing was just baking wedding cakes for an ant hill.

Like Lennon's wail, *I even hate my rock-and-roll!* —
That bleak bus-station howl, and no redemption,
He lost his way and ear for music for a while.

An expense of spirit in a wasted spill,
Like housing frog spawn or a pig sty in a pavilion,
Or distilling fine cognac for a gin mill —

He couldn't shake that nightmare. He could not dispel
The ache of the fake for the sake of composition:
He'd lost his lost language of animal and angel.

All the gorgeous paintings started to unspool,
The world was a panhandler tatterdemalion
Consigning Klees and Monets to a landfill.

The will and wile of art was just a shill,
There was no winged horse, no soaring stallion.
He sickened in his love of poetry, and was ill —
Writing was just icing for an ant hill.

Fields of Sense

Death brings no immediate change of mass.
This shows that life is weightless.
— R. Buckminster Fuller

1.

The freshly dead eyes of a great blue
Dragonfly are the only ones I ever
Saw inside. A compounded riddle —
Reflecting-depth, see-through mirror
Into nothing, silvered blue gelatin.

The corner of my eye, swept by sleep and Spring
And the weekend, showed the dragonfly
To me one Monday morning, dead on its feet
At my feet on the driveway in the path
Of the company trucks. Such finds are a reason —

Neither management nor labor — for getting
To the factory early. The animal
Was uncanny: perfect and without blemish.
It was still early in dragonfly season.
Heart attack? Stroke? Tumor?

On my window sill the eyes turned flat,
Dried away their depth. When the dragonfly
Was finally just the look of itself, it was clear,
And also that insect collections have
No insects in them.

2.

Her friends came carefully to the room where she
Was dying, or wrote her in the room across their
Several distances of miles, good health, and age.
Some just sat, others slept on the couch, keeping
A vigil, breathing the air of sobriety.

When she died the letters en route came untethered,
Faltered a moment — re-addressed themselves to memory.
When she died her face closed, took a passage
That cancelled itself as she went,
Just leaving a head on the pillow.

A dry lake bed is not a place where fishes
Even used to be.

3.

The face is a pool where the world comes
Down to drink, a reflecting depth as wide
As any setting it can take — the kiss,
A broom closet, a sick room, the stars of night.

The front of the head is the place our gaze
Goes down to, the foundation of the pool.
When we look into a face, the world looks
At the world — this is no guarantee of love.

Above the page there is something stirring,
A reach improvises the gravity
Where the mobile of words hangs true,
Is the sky where a poem can be a wing.

Over this page continents of clouds come
And go, the world comes down to drink,
An immense weightless frame composes itself.
It is you, dear reader.